The Passion and Resurrection Narratives of Jesus

STUDY GUIDE

Stephen J. Binz

LITTLE ROCK SCRIPTURE STUDY

A ministry of the Diocese of Little Rock
in partnership with Liturgical Press

Dear Friends in Christ,

The Bible comes to us as both a gift and an opportunity. It is a gift of God who loves us enough to communicate with us. The only way to enjoy the gift is to open and savor it. The Bible is also an opportunity to actually meet God who is present in the stories, teachings, people, and prayers that fill its pages.

I encourage you to open your Bibles in anticipation that God will do something good in your life. I encourage you to take advantage of the opportunity to meet God in prayer, study, and small-group discussion.

Little Rock Scripture Study offers materials that are simple to use, and a method that has been tested by time. The questions in this study guide will direct your study, help you to understand the passages you are reading, and challenge you to relate the Scriptures to your own life experiences.

Allow the Word of God to form you as a disciple of the Lord Jesus. Accept the challenge to be "transformed by the renewal of your mind" (Romans 12:2). Above all, receive God's Word as his gift, and act upon it.

Sincerely in Christ,

✠ J. Peter Sartain
Bishop of Little Rock

Sacred Scripture

"The Church has always venerated the divine Scriptures just as she venerates the body of the Lord, since from the table of both the word of God and of the body of Christ she unceasingly receives and offers to the faithful the bread of life, especially in the sacred liturgy. She has always regarded the Scriptures together with sacred tradition as the supreme rule of faith, and will ever do so. For, inspired by God and committed once and for all to writing, they impart the word of God Himself without change, and make the voice of the Holy Spirit resound in the words of the prophets and apostles. Therefore, like the Christian religion itself, all the preaching of the Church must be nourished and ruled by sacred Scripture. For in the sacred books, the Father who is in heaven meets His children with great love and speaks with them; and the force and power in the word of God is so great that it remains the support and energy of the Church, the strength of faith for her sons, the food of the soul, the pure and perennial source of spiritual life."

Vatican II, Dogmatic Constitution on Divine Revelation, no. 21.

INTERPRETATION OF SACRED SCRIPTURE

"Since God speaks in sacred Scripture through men in human fashion, the interpreter of sacred Scripture, in order to see clearly what God wanted to communicate to us, should carefully investigate what meaning the sacred writers really intended, and what God wanted to manifest by means of their words.

"Those who search out the intention of the sacred writers must, among other things, have regard for 'literary forms.' For truth is proposed and expressed in a variety of ways, depending on whether a text is history of one kind or another, or whether its form is that of prophecy, poetry, or some other type of speech. The interpreter must investigate what meaning the sacred writer intended to express and actually expressed in particular circumstances as he used contemporary literary forms in accordance with the situation of his own time and culture. For the correct understanding of what the sacred author wanted to assert, due attention must be paid to the customary and characteristic styles of perceiving, speaking, and narrating which prevailed at the

time of the sacred writer, and to the customs men normally followed at that period in their everyday dealings with one another."
Vatican II, Dogmatic Constitution on Divine Revelation, no. 12.

Instructions

MATERIALS FOR THE STUDY

This Study Guide: The Passion and Resurrection Narratives of Jesus

Bible: The New American Bible with Revised New Testament or The New Jerusalem Bible is recommended. Paraphrased editions are discouraged as they offer little if any help when facing difficult textual questions. Choose a Bible you feel free to write in or underline.

Commentary: The *Passion and Resurrection Narratives of Jesus: A Commentary* by Stephen J. Binz (The Liturgical Press) is used with this study. The assigned pages are found at the beginning of each lesson.

ADDITIONAL MATERIALS

Bible Dictionary: *The Dictionary of the Bible* by John L. McKenzie (Simon & Schuster) is highly recommended as an additional reference.

Notebook: A notebook may be useful for lecture notes and your personal reflections.

WEEKLY LESSONS

Lesson 1—The Passion According to Mark: Mark 14–15
Lesson 2—The Passion According to Matthew: Matt 26–27
Lesson 3—The Passion According to Luke: Luke 22–23
Lesson 4—The Passion According to John: John 18–19
Lesson 5—The Resurrection According to Mark and Matthew:
        Mark 16, Matt 28
Lesson 6—The Resurrection According to Luke and John:
        Luke 24, John 20–21

SUGGESTED STUDY PLAN

Study Lessons 1–4 prior to Holy Week; study Lessons 5–6 after Easter.

YOUR DAILY PERSONAL STUDY

The first step is prayer. Open your heart and mind to God. Reading Scripture is an opportunity to listen to God who loves you. Pray that the same Holy Spirit who guided the formation of Scripture will inspire you to correctly understand what you read and empower you to make what you read a part of your life.

The next step is commitment. Daily spiritual food is as necessary as food for the body. This study is divided into daily units. Schedule a regular time and place for your study, as free from distractions as possible. Allow about twenty minutes a day. Make it a daily appointment with God.

As you begin each lesson read the assigned chapters of Scripture found at the beginning of each lesson, the footnotes in your Bible, and then the indicated pages of the commentary. This preparation will give you an overview of the entire lesson and help you to appreciate the context of individual passages.

As you reflect on Scripture, ask yourself these four questions:

1. *What does the Scripture passage say?*
   Read the passage slowly and reflectively. Use your imagination to picture the scene or enter into it.

2. *What does the Scripture passage mean?*
   Read the footnotes and the commentary to help you understand what the sacred writers intended and what God wanted to communicate by means of their words.

3. *What does the Scripture passage mean to me?*
   Meditate on the passage. God's Word is living and powerful. What is God saying to you today? How does the Scripture passage apply to your life today?

4. *What am I going to do about it?*
   Try to discover how God may be challenging you in this passage. An encounter with God contains a challenge to know God's will and follow it more closely in daily life.

THE QUESTIONS ASSIGNED FOR EACH DAY

Read the questions and references for each day. The questions are designed to help you listen to God's Word and to prepare you for the weekly small-group discussion.

Some of the questions can be answered briefly and objectively by referring to the Bible references and the commentary *(What does the passage say?)*. Some will lead you to a better understanding of how the Scriptures apply to the Church, sacraments, and society *(What does the passage mean?)*. Some questions will invite you to consider how God's Word challenges or supports you in your relationships with God and others *(What does the passage mean to me?)*. Finally, the questions will lead you to examine your actions in light of Scripture *(What am I going to do about it?)*.

Write your responses in this study guide or in a notebook to help you clarify and organize your thoughts and feelings.

THE WEEKLY SMALL-GROUP MEETING

The weekly small-group sharing is the heart of the Little Rock Scripture Study Program. Participants gather in small groups to share the results of praying, reading and reflecting on Scripture and on the assigned questions. The goal of the discussion is for group members to be strengthened and nourished individually and as a community through sharing how God's Word speaks to them and affects their daily lives. The daily study questions will guide the discussion; it is not necessary to discuss all the questions.

All members share the responsibility of creating an atmosphere of loving support and trust in the group by respecting the opinions and experiences of others, and by affirming and encouraging one another. The simple shared prayer which begins and ends each small group meeting also helps create the open and trusting environment in which group members can share their faith deeply and grow in the study of God's Word.

A distinctive feature of this program is its emphasis on and trust in God's presence working in and through each member. Sharing responses to God's presence in the Word and in others can bring about remarkable growth and transformation.

THE WRAP-UP LECTURE

The lecture is designed to develop and clarify the themes of the lesson. It is not intended to form the basis for the group discussion. For this reason the lecture is always held at the end of the meeting. If several small groups meet at one time, the large group will gather together in a central location to listen to the lecture.

Lectures may be given by a local speaker. They are also available on audio- or video-cassette.

LESSON 1   Mark 14–15
The Passion and Resurrection Narratives of Jesus: A Commentary
pages 9–35

Day 1

1. a) Why is the annual celebration of Holy Week the climax of the Church's year?

   b) What are your favorite memories of Holy Week celebrations?

2. Why are the passion narratives in each of the four Gospels different?

3. How does Mark's Gospel show that the cross is embedded in Jesus' entire life?

Day 2

4. a) What is symbolized by the anointing of Jesus (14:3-8)?

   b) How are the reactions of Jesus' disciples to the woman's anointing of Jesus typical of disciples today (14:4-9)?

5. How could Judas have betrayed Jesus after being so close to him for so long (14:10-11)? (See 14:18-20, 43-45; Pss 41:10; 55:13-15.)

6. Why is it significant that the final events of Jesus' life happen at the feast of Passover (14:1, 12)? (See Exod 12.)

Day 3

7. How does the Old Testament help you to better understand the Eucharist as a community celebration (14:14-16, 22-26)? (See Exod 24:3-8; Jer 31:31-34.)

8. How is the agony in Gethsemane contrasted to the transfiguration (14:32-41)? (See 9:2-13.)

9. What can you learn about human nature and your Christian response from the attitude and actions of the disciples in Gethsemane (14:32-41)?

Day 4

10. a) How must Jesus have felt when all his disciples left him (14:50)?
    b) How do you respond when betrayed or humiliated by friends?

11. What is the temple "not made with hands" that Jesus will build (14:58)? (See Heb 9:11-14; 2 Cor 5:1-5.)

12. What do you see of yourself in the behavior of Peter (14:54, 66-72)?

Day 5

13. What is the difference between the questions posed to Jesus by the high priest (14:61) and by Pilate (15:2)?

14. What elements of the story heighten the sense of abandonment on the cross (15:22-32)?

15. a) How do the words of Psalm 22 foreshadow the scenes of the passion account?
    b) Does Jesus despair on the cross (15:34)?

Day 6

16. In what ways is the death of Jesus associated with the destruction of the Temple (15:38)?

17. Why, at the death of Jesus on the cross, does the centurion proclaim Jesus the Son of God (15:39)?

18. a) How does Joseph of Arimathea show more qualities of true discipleship than the chosen disciples of Jesus (15:43-46)?
    b) Where do you find such faithfulness today?

LESSON 2   Matthew 26–27
The Passion and Resurrection Narratives of Jesus: A Commentary
pages 39–66

Day 1

1. What indications are there that Matthew used Mark as his principal source?

2. Does Jesus indicate that helping the poor is a futile effort (26:11)? (See 19:21; 25:35.)

3. How can greed for money lead to betrayal of people and values (26:15)? (See 6:24; 10:9; 19:23.)

Day 2

4. a) What aspects of the Eucharist are brought out in the narrative of the Last Supper (26:26-30)?
   b) How can each aspect deepen your appreciation of the Eucharist?

5. What causes your faith to be shaken (26:31)?

6. a) What problems or sufferings have you begged God to remove from your life (26:39)?
   b) How might these difficulties fit into God's plan for you?

Day 3

7. a) How does Jesus respond to retaliatory violence (26:51-52)? (See 5:39, 44.)
   b) Does Jesus' rejection of violence have implications for discipleship today?

8. Why does Jesus give an ambiguous response to the high priest when asked about his identity (26:63-64)?

9. How and when do you deny knowing Jesus (26:69-75)? Why?

Day 4

10. a) What is the difference between Peter's denial and Judas' betrayal and their decisions afterwards (26:75; 27:3-5)?
    b) Why would both stories be preserved for the Church?

11. How can spouses (or friends and family members) help one another see the truth of situations clearly (27:19)?

12. a) How does Matthew's Gospel emphasize the dilemma of Pilate and the blame of the Jewish authorities for the death of Jesus (27:15-26)?
    b) To what extent is this emphasis conditioned by the time and circumstances in which Matthew was writing?

Day 5

13. Why is the mockery of Jesus so ironic (27:27-31)?

14. a) How is the final temptation of Christ connected to his earlier desert experience (27:40-43)? (See 4:3-9.)
    b) How does mockery and ridicule tempt you to turn away from your chosen mission?

15. At what key moments does Matthew show Jesus to be the "Son of God" (27:43)? (See 2:15; 3:17; 16:13-16; 17:5.)

Day 6

16. What is symbolized by the opening of the tombs at the death of Jesus (27:51-54)?

17. What significance do you see in the loyalty of the women (27:55-56, 61)?

18. Why is Matthew so careful to explain the seal on the stone and the guard at the tomb (27:62-66)?

LESSON 3   Luke 22–23
The Passion and Resurrection Narratives of Jesus: A Commentary
pages 71–91

Day 1

1. How does the season of Lent encourage you to experience the passion of Jesus more personally?

2. How does the Acts of the Apostles help you understand Luke's Gospel?

3. Why is the passion, death, and resurrection of Jesus called his "exodus" (9:31)?

Day 2

4. What is the significance of Satan in the passion account (22:3, 31-32, 53)? (See 4:13; 10:18.)

5. What does Jesus mean when he tells ut to celebrate the Eucharist "in memory of me" (22:19)? (See Exod 12:14; 1 Cor 10:16-17; 11:24-26.)

6. How does Jesus' discussion of leadership differ from our common understanding of leadership (22:24-27)?

Day 3

7. Why does Jesus tell his disciples that they should now bring a money bag, sack, and sword (22:35-36)?

8. a) How could Peter strengthen others after he denied Jesus (22:31-34, 54-62)? (See Acts 4:8-20; 1 Pet 4:12-19.)
   b) How can you prepare yourself to avoid the danger of denying Jesus in a time of crisis? (See Eph 6:10-17.)

9. In Luke's account of the "Agony in the Garden" (22:39-46), what particular elements impress you? Why?

Day 4

10. Why did Pilate send Jesus to Herod (23:6-7)?

11. In what respects do people still act like Pilate today (23:1-25)?

12. In what ways is Simon, the Cyrenian, an image of discipleship for us (23:26)? (See 9:23; 14:27.)

Day 5

13. What does Jesus mean by saying " . . . if these things are done when the wood is green what will happen when it is dry" (23:31)?

14. What can you learn about Jesus from
    a) his reaction to the mourners (23:27-31)?
    b) his forgiveness of his executioners (23:34)? (See Acts 7:60.)

15. Contrast the reactions of the two criminals crucified with Jesus (23:39-43). Which response to the crucified Jesus is most like your own?

Day 6

16. How does the rending of the temple veil symbolize a fundamental theme of Luke's Gospel (23:45)?

17. How does Psalm 31, prayed by Jesus on the cross, express his attitude at the time of death (23:46)?

18. What events have you witnessed that moved you to sorrow and repentance (23:48)?

LESSON 4   John 18–19
The Passion and Resurrection Narratives of Jesus: A Commentary
pages 99–116

Day 1

1. What elements of the Good Friday liturgy do you remember best?

2. What is the deeper meaning of Jesus' self-identification as "I AM" (18:5-8)? (See 4:26; 6:20; 8:24, 28, 58; 13:19; Exod 3:14.)

3. What is the "cup" which Jesus must drink (18:11)? (See Mark 10:38-39; 14:36.)

Day 2

4. Who was Annas (18:13)? (See 18:19-24.)

5. What emotions must Peter have felt in the courtyard (18:15-18, 25-27)?

6. Why did the Jewish authorities bring Jesus to Pilate (18:31)?

Day 3

7. a) What is the struggle taking place within Pilate during the trial (18:28–19:16)?
   b) How do you experience similar struggles about Jesus within yourself?

8. Why is the truth so often difficult to recognize (18:37-38)?

9. Why does John put the mockery of Jesus at the climactic point of his trial scene (19:1-3)?

Day 4

10. What is the significance of Jesus' death being placed on the Preparation Day for Passover (19:14)? (See 1:29.)

11. Why is the inscription over the cross written in three languages (19:20)?

12. a) What is the significance of the seamless garment (19:23)?
    b) Why is unity, symbolized by the seamless garment, so important for the disciples of Jesus? (See 10:16; 11:52; 17:11, 21-23.)

Day 5

13. How is the mother of Jesus shown to be also the mother of his disciples (19:26-27)? (See 2:1-12; 16:21; Mark 3:31-35; Rev 12:1-18.)

14. Why does John carefully note that the soldiers did not break the legs of Jesus (19:32-33)? (See Exod 12:46; Ps 34:20.)

15. What evidence is there from John's Gospel that the blood and water flowing from Jesus' side represent baptism and Eucharist (19:34)? (See 7:38-39; 6:53-56.)

Day 6

16. How is your discipleship sometimes kept secret like that of Joseph of Arimathea and Nicodemus (19:38-39)? (See 3:2, 21.)

17. In what ways does John's passion account differ from the other accounts?

18. Describe your favorite crucifix and explain what it tells you about Jesus.

LESSON 5   Mark 16 and Matthew 28
The Passion and Resurrection Narratives of Jesus: A Commentary
pages 35–38, 66–70

Day 1 *(Refer to Mark 16.)*

1. a) What are some of the central elements of the Church's Easter Vigil liturgy?
   b) How has this liturgy enhanced your own celebration of resurrection?

2. Why is it significant that only the women discovered the empty tomb (16:1)? (See 15:40-41, 47.)

3. Why does Mark emphasize the discovery of the empty tomb occurring early on the first day of the week (16:2)?

Day 2

4. a) Why does the angel identify the risen Lord as "Jesus of Nazareth, the crucified" (16:6)? (See Commentary, pp. 13–14.)
   b) What does it mean to you to follow a crucified Savior?

5. Why did the Gospel originally end with the promise of Jesus to go before them rather than with his appearances (16:7)?

6. a) Which verse was Mark's ending of the Gospel?
   b) Why did Mark end his Gospel with fear and bewilderment (16:8)?

Day 3

7. Why were other endings added to Mark's Gospel (16:9-20)?

8. Why are the other endings accepted as a canonical part of the Gospel (16:9-20)?

9. What does the empty tomb mean for your life?

Day 4 *(Refer to Matthew 28.)*

10. Why does Matthew not mention that the women were coming to anoint the body of Jesus (28:1)? (See 27:60-61, 66.)

11. Why does Matthew, unlike the other Gospel writers, note the earthquake (28:2)? (See 27:51-54.)

12. a) How is the response of the women in Matthew's account different from that in Mark (28:8)? (See Mark 16:8.)
    b) What would be your response to the angel's message?

Day 5

13. How does Matthew's inclusion of the report of the guard reflect the situation of the Church in his time (28:11-15)? (See 27:62-66.)

14. a) Why is the mountain a particularly significant place for Jesus' final commissioning (28:16)? (See 5:1; 14:23; 15:29; 17:1; Exod 24:12-18; 1 Kgs 19:8-14.)
    b) Have you had any "mountain top" experiences with Jesus?

15. How is the response of the disciples to the risen Jesus characteristic of all Christian disciples (28:17)? Give examples if possible.

Day 6

16. What developing beliefs of the early Church are expressed in the trinitarian formula of baptism (28:19)?

17. In what ways does the Church today carry out its three-fold mission to evangelize, baptize, and teach (28:19-20)?

18. a) How does the final promise of Jesus complete the prophecy given at his birth (28:20)? (See 1:23; Isa 7:14.)
    b) How do you experience the abiding presence of Jesus?

LESSON 6 Luke 24 and John 20–21
The Passion and Resurrection Narratives of Jesus: A Commentary
pages 91–98, 116–127

Day 1 *(Refer to Luke 24.)*

1. How does the question of the angels, "Why do you seek the living one among the dead," challenge the focus of your life (24:5)?

2. Why would the story of the women seem like nonsense to the apostles (24:11)?

3. a) Why did Peter not come to believe when he saw the empty tomb (24:12)?
   b) At what times have you required more evidence in matters of faith?

Day 2

4. At what point did the two disciples at Emmaus recognize Jesus (24:30-31, 35)?

5. How does the Emmaus account express Christ's presence in the liturgy of the Church (24:27-35)?

6. When have the Scriptures caused your heart to burn within you (24:32)? (See Heb 4:12.)

Day 3

7. How does Jesus' appearance to the community of disciples demonstrate that his risen presence is a bodily reality (24:39-43)?

8. a) What is the "promise" which Jesus will send on his disciples (24:49)? (See Isa 32:15; Ezek 36:26-27; Joel 3:1-2.)
   b) How does this promise prepare for the Acts of the Apostles? (See Acts 1:8; 2:33.)

9. What is the role of the ascension of Jesus in Luke's Gospel (24:50-53)?

Day 4 *(Refer to John 20–21)*

10. What is significant about the burial cloths being in the tomb (20:6-7)?

11. a) Why did not Mary Magdalene recognize Jesus (20:14)?
    b) Why did Jesus say to Mary, "Stop holding on to me, for I have not yet ascended to the Father" (20:17)? (See 6:63.)

12. At what moments in your life have you felt that Jesus was truly alive and with you?

Day 5

13. Why is the forgiveness of sins such an important aspect of the Church's mission (20:22-23)? (See 2 Cor 5:18-21; Col 3:12-13.)

14. In what ways are you like Thomas (20:24-29)?

15. What is John's purpose in writing his Gospel (20:30-31)?

Day 6

16. How does the great catch of fish symbolize the life of the Church (21:1-13)?

17. Why is love a prerequisite for pastoral service (21:15-19)?

18. In what sense do you agree with Paul that "if Christ had not been raised, then empty is our preaching; empty, too, your faith" (1 Cor 15:14)?

NOTES